"A fine educator knows and has experienced her material so well that the complex can be made simple. An outstanding educator respects, encourages, and cares for those with whom she works so that they gain support, enthusiasm, and joy from what is being taught. Joyce Merritt is such a teacher/communicator. Her modern-day parables are great gifts for anyone on the spiritual path or searching for it."

Jimmie Webber,
Principal *Putnam County Adult High School*,
Cookeville, TN

NAKED

BEFORE GOD

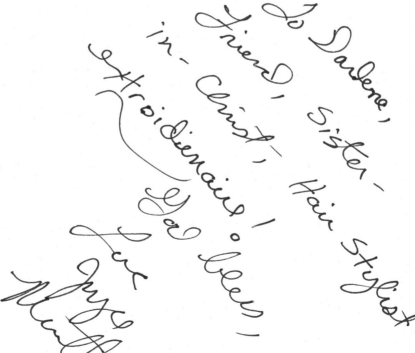

To Darlene,
Friend, Sister –
in – Christ,
Extroidienaus!
God bless,
Luv
Jayce
[signature]

Joyce Merritt

NAKED

BEFORE GOD

A Journey into
Light & Life

TATE PUBLISHING & Enterprises

Naked Before God

This title is also available as a Tate Out Loud product. Visit www. tatepublishing.com for more information.

The opinions expressed by the author are not necessarily those of Tate Publishing, LLC.

Published by Tate Publishing & Enterprises, LLC
127 E. Trade Center Terrace | Mustang, Oklahoma 73064 USA
1.888.361.9473 | www.tatepublishing.com

Tate Publishing is committed to excellence in the publishing industry. The company reflects the philosophy established by the founders, based on Psalm 68:11,
"The Lord gave the word and great was the company of those who published it."

Published in the United States of America

ISBN: 978-1-60604-261-8
1. Christian Living: Personal Growth
08.06.06

CONTENTS

FOREWORD

Joyce Merritt offers a marvelous kaleidoscope of symmetrical loops through her "terrible and wonderful journey into light and life." From her varied roles as wife and mother of five, teacher and pastor, she offers poetic responses to scripture and to life's circumstances. She wrestles with her calling as a contemplative activist—or an activist contemplative—and grants permission to readers to explore their lives through her own freshly-opened eyes.

The distinction between the true and false self dominated Merton's writings, and so, too, Merritt's reflections. Merritt uses various words about a self that is superficial, addicted, encumbered, exterior, illusory, or veiled. For Joyce, the false self does not exist at any deep level of reality but it is what we project from behind walls we construct, consumption, enjoyment, degrees, power, or whatever inhibits us from realizing our identity as God's beloved.

As for the true self, this is what we are: children created in the image and likeness of God for love and self-surrender. Ultimately, as we begin to seek to claim this truest selfhood and journey to transformation, we let go of all the false coverings. This process, however painful, can lead us back to the Holy One.

In an oft-cited passage, Merton recounts his experience around 1958 at the corner of Fourth and Walnut in Louisville, Kentucky—a city! Merton reiterates his belief that the monastic life is not about flight: " ... but the conception of 'separation from the world' that we have in the monastery too easily presents itself as a complete illusion: the illusion that by making vows we become a different species of being, pseudoangels, 'spiritual men,' men of interior life, what have you."

Merton continues, "I have the immense joy of being *man*, a member of a race in which God Himself became incarnate. As if the sorrows and stupidities of the human condition could overwhelm me, now I realize what we all are. And if only everybody could realize this! But it cannot be explained. There is no way of telling people that they are all walking around shining like the sun."[1]

Citing this in her "Reflections of Love," Joyce describes throughout this powerful collection, moments of epiphany. She does so with such insight and integrity that readers are freed to claim their own truest identity, letting go of all that holds them back and coming to be a new person in Christ.

This is God's deepest desire for all God's children. When we walk into light and life, we in turn can make a difference for other companions. One such soul friend on the journey, Joyce offers a web of support and practical guidance into contemplative practices by which we may grow into awareness of our true self.

One need not flee the world in order to live out of this value. The reality of Joyce's life is a way within everyday existence in our world, one in which her dreams resemble those of Merton and monastics of every religious tradition, notably, a world free of the bomb, race hatred, the worst effects of technology (mass media, big business, war, and all the rest), a reality in which, with simplicity uncluttered by the stuff of the world, we participate in the Divine Nature, become one with the God of infinite love, and claim our truest self.

There is no one path to light and life. Like the North American poet Joyce Merritt, Spanish poet

Antonio Machado y Ruiz highlights the image of a journey. "Caminante, no hay camino. Se hace el camino al andar; for those who walk there is no road; the road is made by walking."[2] Like the woman who responded to words in one session, "Misery is optional," may readers join Joyce in a chorus in radical gratitude. Her voice is like a pebble thrown into a pond. I am confident that its ever-widening circle will reach wider and wider. Thanks to God!

Paul R. Dekar,
Memphis Theological Seminary

"Let us present our spirit naked to God."[3]

INTRODUCTION

When my middle son, Joshua, was between two and three years old and reluctantly coming to understand rules and consequences, he despised above all things being revealed in any wrong doing. So he came up with a clever way to deflect that embarrassment. As the moment of truth arrived he would escape to another room and assume an identity of strength and invincibility. Once he came back as Superman. Another time he dressed in my husband's long dragging pants, baggy shirt, and large heavy shoes. He marched heavily and confidently back into the room saying in his best baritone, "Hi. I'm Daddy!" Where no immediate props were available, he improvised. On a family vacation, Josh was trapped at the table of a nice restaurant with several family members, including his new baby brother who was getting all the attention that Josh felt fully entitled to receive. Josh began to act out with typical two-year-old antics and eventually received a reprimand. By then several people were watching and Josh was nearing the point of embarrassment. But where could he run? There was a basket of large, round, bun style rolls on the table. Josh took out a roll and carefully and deliberately placed it directly on top of his head. Family members and restaurant patrons alike tried to stifle grins and to pretend not to notice as Josh moved his bread-topped head slowly and regally from side to side as if he were surveying his kingdom. But we all lost it when he proclaimed clearly, seriously, and with appropriate two-year-old royal authority, "I am the biscuit king."

Though I don't usually wear biscuits on my head, I, too, have caught myself hiding behind the apparent safety of assumed identities. I don't usually make royal proclamations, but I have been known to hide behind a wall of words. I don't normally put on a cape and tights (and we're all thankful for that!), but I sometimes pretend to be superhuman. And at times I can become completely discouraged, disguised in my "incredible shrinking woman" persona, feeling not only less than super human, but indeed, completely superfluous. Help! Which way is better? Which way is real? A favorite preacher friend of mine will often say, "Let's be real." Amen to that. But it's easier said than done, isn't it? Reality is scary. We've been hiding out since that garden incident, afraid of what might be revealed if we let down our guard. So we walk around in fig leaves and fresh baked headgear pretending to live the life we think we probably ought to live. Our pretense can span the gamut from artificially exalted to impossibly worthless depending on what our life circumstances call for. But moments of quiet truth beg the innermost question, *who are we really, aside from external circumstances, expectations, and limitations?* How can we get beyond the pretense and learn to "be real"?

At our core, we all want to "have life to the full" (John 10:10). We suspect that we were created for life that is neither superhuman nor superfluous, but rather life that is real—more real than the circumstances of society that surround us. More real than the circumstances of biology and chemistry that compose us. Ultimately we seek to uncover and rediscover that original gift of life that in its uncorrupted form fills and then transcends all this to be joined to life that is neither superhuman nor superfluous, but in fact, supernatural and eternal. In other words, we seek reunion and relationship with God. In the words of Thomas Merton, "The ego is … real only in relation to its source and end in God."[4]

So why do we put up the barriers? Why the costumes? Why the easy acquiescence to the distractions that separate us from the reality of life connected to God? Like Josh, and me and our parents in the garden, it seems we don't like being found out. There's just stuff about us that we'd rather keep covered up from each other, from God, and perhaps most of all, from ourselves. It's nice to maintain a shiny protective layer that lets everything just roll right off. We loathe to risk coming out of the apparent safety of our protective prisons into the harsh reality of revealing light. The miracle occurs when we realize that we must.

When persons are trapped in deadly addictions, their loved ones will often attempt what has come to be called an "intervention" whereby the person who is headed for destruction is asked and enabled to face the reality of his dangerous state. The hope is that the loved one will be willing to face the light of truth and will thereby open his mind and heart to accept the help required to put him back on the road to life and health.

We who hide and run from reality, we who hide behind fig leaves, magic capes, and walls and veils of every description, we who fear the light of truth even as we crave liberation from darkness, we are in need of an intervention. So our God, the one who loves us most of all, has come to us with the bold and loving intervention of Jesus the Christ. He has come asking and enabling us to face the light of truth that takes us from our paths of destruction to the "way, and the truth and the life" (John 14:6). He says, "Here I am! I stand at the door and knock. If anyone hears my voice and opens the door I will come in and eat with him, and he with me" (Revelation 3:20).

God calls each of us daily, perennially to fullness of life in Christ wherever we are, but how can we hear the call when so many other voices scream for our attention? It is hard to keep up a "resistance to the futile appeals which modern society makes to our senses."[5] So often we are like prodigals, who having started toward home, turn back to heed the squeals of the pig pen, while forfeiting the embrace of our

Father who stands, arms outstretched, awaiting our joyful return to His life-giving embrace.

Once in seminary I was asked as a part of a class exercise to meditate upon the following scripture:

> Simon's mother-in-law was in bed with a fever, and they told Jesus about her. So he went to her, took her hand and helped her up. The fever left her and she began to wait on them.
>
> That evening after sunset the people brought to Jesus all the sick and demon-possessed. The whole town gathered at the door, and Jesus healed many who had various diseases. He also drove out many demons, but he would not let the demons speak because they knew who he was. *Very early in the morning, while it was still dark, Jesus got up, left the house and went off to a solitary place, where he prayed.* Simon and his companions went to look for him, and when they found him, they exclaimed: "Everyone is looking for you!"
>
> Mark 1:30–35

I read over and meditated upon this scripture for some time. And then, of all the possible points I could have taken from that passage, the one sentence that burned in my heart and mind was "*Very early in the morning, while it was still dark, Jesus got up, left the house and went off to a solitary place, where he prayed.*" On that particular day, I had come to class (a five-hour drive one way from Cookeville to Memphis, Tennessee) through a literal fog of the atmosphere and a figurative fog of the mind. I'd been to the dentist the day before for a root canal—my true idea of horror. Then, I found my beloved cat dead in our yard for no apparent reason. And the dental drugs were not wearing off as they should have. I was exhausted and had to stop and sleep along the way. This made me late, which is something I hate to be. I read that scripture and I thought, *Wow. Jesus took time to be still and alone with God. He took time to gather strength even when the world was clawing for more of Him.* It was like a light shining into my fog with the truth that, "You can do that too!" I think I'd forgotten how to "be still and know that (God) is God" (Psalm 46:10) and I am not. That struck me as really good news.

Jesus regularly took time away from the pull of the world to seek quiet communion with the Father. Jesus knew how to be still, quiet, and open to God even in the midst of loud and difficult circumstances—*especially* in the midst of loud and difficult circumstances.

When we place our open hearts and minds and whole selves before God with reverent expectation, we become open to the truth and light that God offers His children. At first it is hard to step into that light. We are vulnerable without our veils and costumes. For in the light of this communion, we come to see with greater clarity, the vast gulf that looms between ourselves and Holy God.[6] We seek, thereby, to die to the self that is apart from God, in order to live in union within God, and God within us, so that "Wherever ye turn, there is the face of God … (and) everything shall perish but His face."[7] As we journey toward achievement of this inner communion of God with the inner "naked self" we begin to live in the resurrected fullness of life for which we were originally created: so "That (we) may have life and have it to the full" (John 10:10).

From the early fathers and mothers of the church to Christians of today, those who seek to live an authentic life immersed in the reality of God have suggested a common order to the progression of stages through which the seeker passes on the way to the Father. We might think of these stages of progression as land-marks along the Way.

The first step is the dawning light of *truth*. Standing in the honest light of truth, the seeker realizes that he must let go of all that is false, all that creates a barrier between himself and the revealing light of Holy God. That letting go of what has seemed like self-protection and self-sufficiency is a necessary spiritual death. But this *death* (or conviction as it is sometimes called) enables the newly cleansed spirit to look up from his honest state of humility and see the hand of God waiting there to raise him up to new life—real life, reborn life. And this is *resurrection*. This is the Easter experience that God grants to every one of his children who will be reborn into the real life that He gives. This is the glorious awakening of the soul when "the day dawns and the morning star rises in your hearts" (2 Peter 1:19). Resurrection leads to the real and abundant life that Jesus the Christ has promised to all who will receive: "I have come that they may have life, and have it to the full" (John 10:10). As that real *life* fills and transforms us, we become ever more aware of our need for the light and truth of God. So we continue on an upward cycle of life.

May we open our eyes, our hearts, our hands, and our lives to the light of truth. May we let go of the false coverings and the distractions that separate us from the source of life. May we grow hungry and thirsty and may we be filled with the Spirit Who creates us and sustains us. Let us with bold humility present our spirits naked before God so that finally, fully, and eternally we can live.

CHAPTER 1

TRUTH

The first step on the journey to life that is real and eternal could be described as recognition and acceptance of reality, in one word, *truth*. Once one has fully arrived at this landmark, the light of truth exposes and convicts, even as it offers hope for healing and redemption. And so, the one who stands in the truth of God, must accept his conviction, which leads to his cleansing. This is the dilemma of seeing and getting beyond one's illusory self in order to remove the veils that further separate our vision from divine light, "the veils or coverings that impede the direct, naked sensitivity by which the spirit touches the Divine Being." When the light of this truth is offered us, we must "accept the graces that console and graces that humiliate us" as we guard against the natural tendency to "desensitize our souls so we can't perceive graces we foresee as painful."[8] In the words of St. Augustine, "They love the truth as it brings light. They hate it as it brings reproof." [9] But it is in this revealed recognition of our fallen state that we come to recognize the "holy thirst" that will allow us no peace until it is quenched.[10] It is through our acceptance of exposure to this new light that we may, with God's help, come to remove the false layers of deception and masks in order to uncover that deep self that is the true self, created in God's image.[11] And from that terrible and wonderful position of truth we are finally able to be rejoined with the source of all life and truth. For ever since we first turned away from that Source until now, our souls have cried out for *reunion*.

"Your true identity is as a child of God." [12]

REUNION

In the beginning, God created humanity in God's own image, a beloved extension of God's own life in the glorious garden of His creation, where God and His children could enjoy the life of God forever.

But humanity was soon distracted and enticed away from God, who communed with them at their very core that was His own image, and toward the things God had created, which were very lovely, but entirely external to themselves. They tried, by consumption and enjoyment of the lovely created things, to fill themselves up from the outside in. They seemed to enjoy bringing the external things in, but no matter how much they consumed, they were never truly satisfied. They became so dissatisfied within themselves that they sought to cover up in order to disguise the unsatisfactory, hungry, lonely beings they perceived themselves to be. When God called for them, they turned away from His communion in shame. And so, apart from the inner life that He provided, they began to die (just as He had told them they would, when He created them and gave them that choice).

Finally, some of humanity realized that they were

not going to be able to achieve life or even overcome death by consumption, enjoyment, or intellect. So they began to call out to their Creator God, who alone could provide the inward life for which they were created and without which they suffered death. They began to cry out to God to deliver them from death (that was separation from life in union with God, who had created them a beloved extension of His own life within creation itself).

So God, who had made humanity in His image, made Himself to be also in humanity's image, the image of the Son, so that he could enter into the creation that He had made, and through humanity itself, draw all His children back into full communion with Him. Making Himself in the image of humanity, which had freely chosen death for itself, God had thereby chosen to endure that same death and in so doing, He opened the door between the life of God and the death of humanity, a clear passage for all to enter into.

And this door, God the Son, Jesus Christ, opens even now, through God the Spirit, to all who would seek reunion with God through spiritual re-creation and return to the life giving communion, which offers true life now and forever in the garden of God's love.

"The Ego is ... real only in relation to its source and end in God."[13]

Have you ever hidden from the light? The truth of dressing room fluorescent lighting is something that causes me to cringe and crave a darker, more flattering form of illumination. Actually, what I want is *less* illumination. In a similar way, it's not altogether gratifying to see oneself in God's full light illumination. It's tempting to run to the more flattering shadows of worldly standards. There are always ways and means to elicit comforting shades of worldly honor and praise, believing for a time that this is better because it feels better. But as we slide down into the darkness of superficial recognition, flattery, and lies, we will (hopefully) realize that something is missing. We crave the very light of truth that we shunned. And, in fact, we wither from the inside out until we can reconnect with that light and life that is both our Source and our purpose.

THE SOURCE

A jewel shone in the dull brown earth
The clear lake of the sun,
Nourished by three bubbling springs,
An oasis of rejuvenation.
Life joined the lake and filled the lake,
And surrounded in circles of green,
Led by the light reflected below
From the powerful source above.
In grateful praise the lake looked up,
So those who had gathered turned also toward the sun.
The circles increased with abundant life,
Until confusion turned some to the lake.
Their praise of the lake's reflected light
Cast shadows that blocked out the sun.
The lake's life decreased
As his inner light dimmed.
For the lake saw no sun
In the shadows of their praise.
The waters were clear in the three springs alone
Where life could dwell and sunlight shone.

Our life should always be seen in the light of the Cross. The Passion, Death and Resurrection of Christ the Lord have entirely changed the meaning and orientation of man's existence and of all that he does. One who cannot realize this will spend his life building a spider's web that has no substance and no real reason for existence.[14]

Ultimately, we were created by God for God and for one another. But in the shadows of our fear of exposure we lost sight of both our life Source and our life orientation. Nevertheless, God loved us still. So he sent the light of truth to come into our midst, walking the way, lighting the way, and even becoming the way to truth and life.

He was in the world, and though the world was made through Him, the world did not recognize Him. He came to that which was His own, but His own did not receive Him. Yet to all who received Him, to those who believed in His name, He gave the right to become children of God—children born not of natural descent, nor of human decision or a husband's will, but born of God. The Word became flesh and made His dwelling among us. We have seen His glory, the glory of the One and Only, who came from the Father, full of grace and truth.

John 1: 10–14

His name is Jesus. He leads us through the terrible truth of the cross, through the valley of the shadow of death, and on to the glorious light and life of his resurrection. Those who walk in His way must step boldly into the terrible and wonderful way of truth and light that brings us into connection with God and with one another.

UNMADE WEB

Too much to say, no time to hear.
Commitments let nobody near.
Ideas to show, too tired to see.
No time to spare, even for me.
Acquaintances, yet none a friend.
My heart drops to a lonely end.
A web pushed out, pushed out in air
With no touch points to hold it there
A loose and lonely, dangling free,
Exercise in futility.

"When he saw the crowds, he had compassion on them, because they were harassed and helpless, like sheep without a shepherd" (Matthew 9:36).

When we step into the truth and realize our connection to another, we may be shaken by the reality of what we see and what we are compelled to do. Those who were once comfortably invisible to us suddenly become real. We are drawn with a growing sense of responsibility and even love for those who we once could have easily stepped over without stirring the inconvenient pangs of concern or the troublesome requirement for a call to action. We *see* the need and know our responsibility to it. We also see that this connection and this concern could easily overwhelm us. But then we remember that we are not alone. We have the combined strength and capabilities of each other. And we have the unlimited power of God. Wow. That changes everything.

MISERY OPTIONAL

Christmas was near. The school holiday was only days away. Roberta sat at the table together with other single mothers, working on their daily journal entry for the adult education class. The teacher had written what she considered a clever "story starter" on the board. This was the phrase: *"Pain is inevitable but misery is optional."*

"What does this mean to you?" she asked the class. She thought this would be a "glass-is-half-full" kind of topic. She really searched for these sorts of topics since classes so often seemed to degenerate into woeful commiseration sessions among the poor, under-educated, and normally single young mothers in the program. As the class began to discuss what this phrase might mean, a lovely, quiet, auburn-haired teen mother named Roberta spoke up with confidence. She knew the answer to this one, "That means suicide."

The teacher recognized in her face that Roberta was not saying this for any sort of shock value, but simply assuming that this would be the obvious answer to all. So the teacher responded, "Ah. Explain what you mean."

Roberta smiled indulgently and answered, "Well,

you know you're going to have pain and misery in life. But you have the option of suicide. That may be painful, but at least it gets you out of the misery." The teacher and the students alike received Roberta's understanding of the phrase. And the class continued. But all present had heard a revelation about the quiet, sweet, pretty Roberta.

Everyone began to listen very carefully to all her life was revealing. The cries for help became audible. Eventually, she had enough trust in others and confidence in herself to get out of a genuinely suicidal existence wherein she was essentially being held captive in domestic and sexual slavery to three young men running from the police in other states. She was caring for her infant daughter and had become pregnant again. Her concern for her two babies overcame her own mortal fear. Several community churches and emergency organizations worked with us to get her safely and secretly out of the situation and out of the state to a place where a family member had a home and a job waiting for her.

Misery is optional. Dear Lord, we need your help.

When we look to the Lord who calls us to follow in His way, we wonder, Can it be true? Can He really be who He says he is? How can I know for sure?

"Jesus Christ, Jesus Christ

Who are you? What have you sacrificed?

Jesus Christ, Jesus Christ

Who are you? What have you sacrificed?

Jesus Christ, Superstar

Do you think you're what they say you are?

Jesus Christ, Superstar

Do you think you're what they say you are?"

Lyrics from *Jesus Christ Superstar*

GOD, NAKED BEFORE US

God has come naked before us, stripped of glory,
We stripped Him of humanity,
Peering underneath,
Like a child stripping a new, unknown doll,
We sought the naked truth
Of what You are
And the Substance that lay exposed
Even at the naked core
Was the same substance that we had seen
On the surface,
The substance of absolute love.

> Love is announced and "instilled," but it is equaled with obedience and conformity within the framework of an impersonal corporation. This means that in practice love is overshadowed by intolerance, suspicion and fear. Authority becomes calculating and anxious. . . . The church is preached as a communion, but is run, in fact, as a collectivity, and even as a totalitarian collectivity.[15]

"The easy way out is to take the package deal. To let religious formulas substitute for spirituality. To allow others to digest our God for us."[16]

The light of truth strikes each of us individually as well as all who come to the light collectively. When joining with God and one another in the light of Christ, we become ever more aware of the truth that illuminates our path. As we are transformed by that light, we are compelled to carry it into a dark world. Woe to us if we, once having the light, should then retreat into the apparent comfort of the ever-present shadows that tempt us to live not in the liberation of God's light, but in the dark motivations of fear and *self-* preservation.

"Some Pharisees who were with him heard him say this and asked, 'What? Are we blind too?'

Jesus said, 'If you were blind, you would not be guilty of sin; but now that you claim you can see, your guilt remains'"

(John 9:41).

SERMONS AND WEAPONS

They filed in deliberately, greeted each other sedately, and prepared for their weekly edification. He frowned down from the pulpit as he began to systematically list and condemn the various promoters of evil and their degrading influence upon society. He lamented that church members were found associating with these corrupting forces. He filled the awed followers with fear of the forces that would swallow the world and them in it. He sent them running down the aisle to beg for their personal safety from an evil world.

When they left, they were worried and depressed. Soon they discussed ways to barricade themselves from the world. They learned to apprehend evil and shun it. They erected a wall against corruption. But still they feared. They sought new defenses against the pursuing evil. The weapons were easily gotten and they amassed arsenal. Their inventory registered the weaponry by such names as righteousness, piety, conservatism, realism, regulation, uniformity, and religion. (These were only code names. Their covert leader held the actual identifications. They were self-righteousness, selfishness, elitism, cynicism, narrow-mindedness, prejudice, and hate.) They could not overcome evil. It seemed logical to escape it, with barricades firmly in place.

Long ago another group assembled for a sermon.

They gathered erratically, outdoors on a hillside. They came from all walks of life to hear this man who offered hope. Young, old, children, beggars, and rich men assembled as He sat to speak.

He looked at the crowd with eyes that said I love you. Then He spoke of familiar and wonderful things. He talked about love, happiness, and hope. He said the last would be first, the meek exalted. He taught forgiveness and forbearance. He said to love unconditionally. And they hungered and thirsted for more. He gave them food for their bodies and food for their spirits.

When He left them, they talked excitedly of His new way and the hope He had given. Then they shared His message with others who were hurting like they had been. But the light of truth He brought revealed evil in the darkness, so many sought to put out the light. And they did. (They thought.) But He rose up from death, still loving those who had killed Him, having died for those very persons who took His life. He offered to share this eternal life with any who would face and put to death the evil in their hearts. Then He sent them into the face of the world's evil like lambs among wolves, but armed with a weapon that no force, not even death, could overcome: His Love. He said, "In the world you will have tribulation. But be of good cheer. I have overcome the world" (John 16:33, NKJV).

"We are a people who lack awareness!"[17]

In the light of truth, we must come to recognize that God has blessed us with many gifts that we are to use in His light, for His glory, and thereby ultimately for our own good. But in our chosen state of blindness, how often do we cut off our own noses to spite our faces, bringing ruin to that which we have been given, even the earth itself, for the promise of immediate gratification? The light of truth compels us to see that our selfish acts are short sighted. Otherwise, we may discover with sadness and regret that we have despised our birthright for a pot of stew.

Once when Jacob was cooking some stew, Esau came in from the open country, famished. He said to Jacob, "Quick, let me have some of that red stew! I'm famished!" (That is why he was also called Edom.)

Jacob replied, "First sell me your birthright."

"Look, I am about to die," Esau said. "What good is the birthright to me?"

But Jacob said, "Swear to me first." So he swore an oath to him, selling his birthright to Jacob.

Then Jacob gave Esau some bread and some lentil stew. He ate and drank, and then got up and left. So Esau despised his birthright.

Genesis 25: 29–34

OBLIVION

Why is it some men need the land
To smell and feel and till the land
And where abused, to heal the land
With warm caress of rugged hand?
My grandfather drew from the land.
His careful life grew from the land,
Umbilically a two-way cord
Through which he took and then restored.
Why is it some men hate the land,
Auspiciously reshape the land,
While viciously they rape the land,
Then hate the ground that soiled their hand?
They leave her covering agape;
And sneer at their successful rape.
Her riches are all theirs to take
Without regard for what's at stake.
I hear the bulldozers approaching,
Cold barren concrete, fast encroaching,
Dead scents of cash here in my hand
Have sterilized the smell of land.

In the light of truth, we may see it revealed that persons who we had once conveniently judged to be unworthy of our concern are, in fact, in the greatest need of our concern. Whereas the comfort of our dark unknowing allowed us to hold on to settled and self-serving prejudice, the light of truth will illuminate the injustice of our past blindness and call us further to seek the justice to which God has always called His children.

He has showed you, O man, what is good.
And what does the LORD require of you?
To act justly and to love mercy
And to walk humbly with your God.

Micah 6:8

ABANDONED

"Danny, Danny Clark!"

Danny slowly raised his deep black eyes above his paperback western and glared into the angry, tired face of Mrs. McAllister. "Danny, you can either put away your book and join this class, or join Mr. Howard in the principal's office." Danny looked smugly around at the expectant faces of his classmates, shrugged his shoulders, picked up his book, and strode slowly out of the room.

Mrs. McAllister took a deep breath, called the class back to order, and continued absentmindedly with the day's reading worksheet. She'd given up on the boy. If he didn't make it to the principal's office, she'd report his class walkout and he would be suspended. Again. She'd be temporarily free of his contaminating, self-willed attitude. Then after a few more inevitable suspensions, he'd be expelled. Then they'd be rid of him for good.

Danny started to go to the principal's office and tell him just what he thought of Mrs. McAllister and every other teacher at the school. He'd be suspended anyway. But he was tired. He just walked home. It was easier.

His grandmother called from her chair in the darkened living room, "Danny, is that you?" "Yes, Granny," he called, stepping carefully across the rotting floorboards near the front door. He had unsuccessfully tried to repair the leaks in the porch extension of the old house's deteriorating roof. He'd have to try again. Granny would surely fall when the boards eventually gave away.

"You're home early," she called over her shoulder without moving from her transfixed position in the flickering light of her television reality.

"Yea. Today's a short day, Granny, teacher workday."

"Oh, all right. Do your homework."

"Yes ma'am."

Danny opened the kitchen junk drawer, reached in the back, and took out his clip. Then he found the stub of his last joint in his shirt pocket and went to the backyard to smoke it. His grandmother was involved with her "stories" and wouldn't move until the theme music of "General Hospital" ended her weekday dramas. They were more real to her than her grandson, whom she often called "Trey" after the young doctor on "All My Children."

Danny put the empty clip into his pocket and took out his paperback. It was quiet and peaceful in the backyard and he could escape completely into the western frontier. Danny knew he'd been born too late. He liked to imagine making his own way on some untamed stretch of wilderness where his restless independence would have been an asset. He loved the portrait of the unattached American cowboy, riding off into the sunset. That was him, born too late.

As Danny dissolved into the West, he was herding the cattle across some hilly terrain. He and the other cowboys were circling back, pulling the stragglers to keep them in the forward-moving herd. But some of the stragglers refused to be herded. They went off in their own direction, despite the best efforts of the … teachers? The cowboy's faces were those of his teachers and the cattle were the students. Now Danny was one of the stragglers. But the cowboys had to turn away from them and give them up for the good of the rest of the herd. The majority of the cattle were herded on past, over the steep ridge. The few stubborn, ornery stragglers were left behind, some alone, and some in small groups to fend for themselves. Abandoned now, they could make the effort to catch up on their own or suffer the consequences of their stubbornness. One young, exhausted bull was immediately set upon by hungry wolves who'd been trailing the herd, waiting for just such an opportunity. A couple of steers ran after the dust kicked up by the main herd. Danny stood there, alone in the dust, surveying the bleak horizon, when he began to shake. What was happening?

He looked up and there was Granny, shaking his arm, looking very old. "Danny, come inside. It's almost dark. I need you to run to the market for some TV dinners." Danny roused himself from his strange dream and helped his hobbling granny back inside. He turned on the lights in the dark house, got Granny some coffee and a blanket, and turned on "The Wheel of Fortune." Then he took the money from the cookie jar and walked out the door.

"It is simply taken for granted that, since the white man is superior, the Negro wants to become the white man. And we, liberals and Christians that we are, advance generally with open arms to embrace our little black brother and welcome him into white society."[18]

Growing up on a farm, I saw the truth about animal society. Animals are not humane. Farm animals and wild animals are not naturally giving or embracing of one another. They are basically self-centered and their social interactions are designed for self-protection—especially chickens. Chickens do not like to accept newcomers. Put a bird who is new and different in with a settled flock, and that newcomer is in for a terrible hazing to say the least. In fact, unless given some outside protection and time to acclimate, the new bird may be pecked and spurred to death. Chickens are not supposed to be humane, however; they are not human. What's our excuse?

MICROCOSM

He lies here dead whose color, wrong,
With haughty gait and too brash song,
Outcast, had tried to penetrate;
Thus leading to his current state.
His kind will find their life here hard,
In microcosmic poultry yard.

"The rule of Benedict tells us to accept our personal weaknesses, to see them as the road to humility and community, and to stay the course, no matter the tide."[19]

I once preached a sermon on humility. A visiting preacher met me at the door and asked, "If a person was truly humble, would you know it?" Interesting point. We can't be proud or assertive about our humility can we? As we step into the light of God's truth, we find that we really haven't come quite as far as we thought we had. And then, we have to step a bit further into that blinding, but glorious light.

For by the grace given me I say to every one of you: Do not think of yourself more highly than you ought, but rather think of yourself with sober judgment, in accordance with the measure of faith God has given you.

Romans 12:3

REVEALED IN SILENCE

I was thinking on the most recent enlightenment that I had gained in this experience of monastic silence. I pondered the idea that we (I in particular) tend to hide behind a wall of words. We explain, justify, and excuse ourselves to others, to ourselves, and—we think, perhaps—to God. We seem to be saying, "Oh, I know it may appear that I am thus, but if you'll only listen to my explanation, you'll see that I am much better, much more cultured, much wiser, and much purer than that." Perhaps we fool ourselves and maybe we fool "some of the people some of the time," but God sees us as we are all of the time.

It occurred to me that in silence, if you do something stupid or rude or inappropriate, the deed is just there. It is done. No comment need be made. No penalty. No praise. No excuses. Silence can make one quite vulnerable. At first, the silent situation made me feel self-conscious, aware of my vulnerable self just "out there" with no words to protect me: no distracting story, no witty catch line to draw approval or distract from my real, exposed presence. *What an insight!* I thought, *I'm getting pretty good at this "naked before God" stuff.*

I sat closely between two silent meal companions, enjoying my wisdom. I imagined how enlightened I would sound when I shared this new insight. I swallowed my water in my quiet state of advanced illumination, and up it came for all to hear. I burped. And as we were in silence, I couldn't joke about it, feign false humility, beg pardon, or really even laugh out loud at myself. I glanced side to side at my companions. Had they heard? It was sort of an inward burp. I thought I saw the twinkle of a repressed smile in their eyes as they politely stared straight ahead.

Oh well. There is no taking it back. No words to disguise the crude reality that Joyce is a burper. God has a very pointed sense of humor. (Thanks be to God!)

"Reveal Your Presence,
And may the vision of Your Beauty be my death;
For the sickness of love
Is not cured
Except by your very Presence and Image"

St. John of the Cross[20]

CHAPTER 2

DEATH

The light of truth brings us to the point where we are compelled to enter into the terrible, liberating process of having our false layers removed, our worldly encumberments released. This is the next landmark on the journey to real life. Whatever separates us from the true life that God gives must be put to *death*.

Death is the point at which the inner true self in the image of God sheds the external "fictitious character active self-impersonation" along with all the false coverings and worldly trappings that hide the naked self from the terrible and wonderful gaze of God. [21] In so doing, the externally rich man sheds his illusory wealth, and comes clean and free through the narrow "eye of the needle" that is both death and the gateway to life–the very Person of Christ (Matthew 19: 24). The externally encumbered man who becomes aware of his intolerable burden, heavy with the cares and self-centered concerns of the flesh, is compelled to leave his burden at the gate and to enter into the fold of the Shepherd who offers him safe passage through the valley of the shadow to the green pastures and still waters of life that is full to overflowing (Psalm 23).

"Again I tell you, it is easier for a camel to go through the eye of a needle than for a rich man to enter the kingdom of God."

Matthew 19:24

THROUGH THE EYE OF THE NEEDLE

He had everything he could ever want.
What a fortunate child.

He was poised to grow into the riches
his parents could provide.
What a hopeful child.

He grew into a young man who strove
to do everything right.
What a good child.
So he lived in the fluorescent light
of the riches he had plucked from the world.
What a fortunate man.

He did all he was supposed to,
and by sheer will and the sweat of his brow,
he lived the American dream.
What a solid citizen.

Troubles never came his way—well if they did,
he just let them slide right off his shiny veneer.
What a smooth man.

In times of quiet, when he wondered just who he was,
he looked at the wealth around him for comfort.
What a rich man.

"He doesn't need for anything," said the world.
"I am hungry for more," said the rich man.
And he grasped all he could gather to feed his hunger.
What a motivated man.

He had little time to waste.
He seized the day with abandon.
What a focused man.

The world said, "He has made himself a glorious life."
The man said, "I followed all the rules.
I have everything.
I have done everything
And still I hunger. There is no point to any of this."
What a tragic man. Give him some drugs.

He spent all he had to cope with his illness
and he became poor. The world said,
"What man?"

The man said,
"What man?"

God said,
"What a fortunate child.

Come now through the eye
of the needle and into my love."
And the man smiled.

"We must learn to follow our own call."[22]

Must we really let go of the things we enjoy, the people we love, and the supports that we have relied upon in order to answer God's call? Why should we have to let go of what we so fondly hold on to in order to follow the One who holds us? How could Jesus have expected the rich young ruler to leave it all behind in order to follow Him?

> Peter said to him, "We have left everything to follow you!"
>
> "I tell you the truth," Jesus replied, "no one who has left home or brothers or sisters or mother or father or children or fields for me and the gospel will fail to receive a hundred times as much in this present age (homes, brothers, sisters, mothers, children and fields—and with them, persecutions) and in the age to come, eternal life. But many who are first will be last, and the last first."
>
> Mark 10: 28–31

WEDNESDAY'S MEDITATION

Lord God,
What do you ask of me?
I feel your pull.
I hear your call.
I answer yes into the darkness,
And yet I fear the unknown
Into which I must trust myself
Fully into your care.
You have sheltered me under your wings.
You have promised to ever shelter me.
Why do I fear?
To what are you calling me?
From what are you calling me?
I fear most that which I must leave behind.
Turn me not into a pillar of salt.
I will trust your leading.
Give me ears to hear you, my Shepherd.
Lead me into the green pastures, still waters,
And even through the valley of the shadow of
death.
Lord Jesus, I ask you,
Am I running to you or away from you?

Why am I keeping you at bay?

I don't consciously desire to be separate from you.

And yet fear burns low and slow in my belly.

I will make an idol of nothing.

You are my God,

Not my children.

You are my God,

Not my spouse.

You are my God,

Not my parents.

You are my God,

Not my friends.

You are my God,

Not my job.

You are my God,

Not those who come to me in need.

And yet,

I serve you best when I serve even the least of these.

I love you most when I love the least of these.

I come truly into your presence

when I commune with even the least of these.

May I serve you joyfully.

May I love you completely.
May I enter into full communion with You
And with all of Your creation.
Amen.

THE 23RD PSALM: A PERSONAL ADAPTATION

God is my leader and full provision for life,
So I will never be lacking in anything that I need.
He brings me to a place of rest, comfort, and peace,
Where He fills my thirsty soul with refreshing, cool, everlasting streams of living water.
Because my leader, provider, and sustainer is God,
He always points me in the right direction. I hear His voice and follow Him.
When evil and dark forces surround me, I will not be afraid,
Because you, my God, are with me, holding me close to your love
And holding the evil that surrounds me at bay.
I am safe and comforted in your complete embrace.
You celebrate our communion of life in joy,
Even in the midst of evil that would come against me.
You have selected me to be yours,

And the joy of that knowledge fills my heart to overflowing.
So that I know that I will live with you in your goodness and mercy forever.

Once upon a time some seekers from the city asked the local monastic a question:

"How does one seek union with God?" And the Wise One said, "The harder you seek, the more distance you create between God and you." "So what does one do about the distance?" the seekers asked. And the elder said simply, "Just understand that it isn't there."[23]

As we seek to become unburdened of our self-serving worldly attachments, perhaps the hardest thing to release is our need to understand with the mere logic of human ingenuity, the way that leads to communion with God and life to the full. For in fact, it seems that God confounds the plans of men in order to demonstrate the power that is clearly beyond the ways and means of any mortal person, no matter how gifted. However lofty or noble our intentions may be in our attempts to orchestrate holiness, we discover that we can't plan it. We can't force it. We can't even fully understand it. At the end of it all, it seems we simply have to trust God and receive it. How amazing that God calls us first to simply "Be still and know that (God) is God" (Psalm 46:10) and realize that living in this truth is more than enough.

THE WALLS OF JERICHO

Lord, I seek the Promised Land.

I thirst from my desert sojourn.

I hunger for the abundance of your promised milk
and honey.

Yet the walls separate me from your presence,

The Jericho walls of my striving.

I march around the periphery, but I cannot enter in.

You say:

"Stop striving, keep marching."

I'll march, but that makes no sense.

"Stop striving, keep marching."

I'll obey. But this is silly.

"Stop striving, keep marching."

I will obey. When do I get in?

"Stop striving, keep marching."

I will obey and trust your timing.

"Stop striving, keep marching."

I will obey and that is enough.

"Stop striving, keep marching."

I will obey for just as long as it takes.

"Stop striving, keep marching."

I will march for you forever.

"Sound the trumpet and enter."
The walls are tumbling down!

What do you think? If a man owns a hundred sheep, and one of them wanders away, will he not leave the ninety-nine on the hills and go to look for the one that wandered off? And if he finds it, I tell you the truth, he is happier about that one sheep than about the ninety-nine that did not wander off. In the same way your Father in heaven is not willing that any of these little ones should be lost.

Matthew 18: 12–14

How very hard it is to face the death of our own self-conceived righteousness: That is, the idea that our holy search and eager attempts to be good and pleasing to God somehow make us better or more deserving of God's grace than others who seem less holy than we imagine we are. But if we truly stand in the light of truth we will begin to recognize, and by the mercy of God put to death, the ugliness of our own conceit as it is revealed in God's holy and glorious grace.

BILL: THE CASE FOR HELL

Today I watched the ashes of a sad person buried. Bill's family, who had endured his sad existence, sat and watched at the graveside. Perhaps they had been a part of his misery. He had surely been a part of theirs. He had lived very little in the last years of his life. He had been intentionally killing himself for years with alcohol. When that death was taken from him in jail, he attempted death with ropes of sheets. That failing, he found another way to embrace death after returning home from his incarceration. He shot himself in his home with his wife and five children present. He had been a veteran. He was given the honor afforded that service to country.

I never knew him to serve anyone other than himself. Outwardly and from my vantage point, he had done nothing, accomplished nothing worthy of honor. He had been a poor, even abusive, father and husband. He had shown no respect for any laws that had inconvenienced him. He eagerly sought to father children but did not seek to support them. He lived the last couple of years off his oldest son's disability check … a disability fostered mainly in this child due to his father's constant, merciless, emotional abuse. I've heard that the man had a warm and tender side. But I never saw it. I saw someone hiding from his responsibilities, someone who deserved neither pity nor mercy.

At the graveside, as the minister spoke about how he touched the lives of his family, I wanted to scream, He touched them all right. He made their lives a living hell, and now that's just what he's enduring! The whole idea of hell and justice seemed so appropriate at this point. I was saddened for the trauma of his family. But I could not muster one thought of mercy for his soul. I could not imagine a single regret that I had failed to speak to him about the love of Christ and the road to life. All I could think was, He had the chance. He refused to take it. He deserves whatever he gets. Maybe God will be merciful. But this sure seems like the clear case for justice.

The thought that God loved every son and daughter and would not wish that any should perish crossed my mind. But I could not take that thought to heart. Surely God could not love him?! Bill had crashed and burned his wife's photo of Christ and her Bible after they were married. He refused to try to turn his life around. He deserved death. And I could not be sad. How could God be sad?

And then, the great gulf between my own unworthiness and God's holiness loomed before me. And it looms before me now—a chasm that I can't cross except that I be taken across. I remembered that God, who loves Bill fully as much as me, will not force us to travel the Way to life that spans the chasm looming between our unworthy selves and God's glory. But rather, God gives everything—His very self and life—to bring us to the full life of eternal communion with God and with one another in spite of our rejection—because of our rejection. God already went to hell and back again for Bill, my brother. And I had stopped dead in my tracks at the prison door. Forgive me, God. Forgive us. A clear case—for mercy.

"Then suddenly we saw him no more. He was in white … the waters had closed over his head, and he was submerged in the community."[24]

I went to a monastery to meet with God. My schedule was tight. I had three days and nights for God to speak to me. I came. Unpacked. Waited. Nothing. Said my prayers. Still nothing. Went for a walk. Nothing. Nothing. Nothing! *Where are you God? I'm waiting.* Then I realized that I had been so long moving through life without stopping to be refilled by God's Spirit that I was like a near-empty reservoir in great need of refilling. And I was making that task harder with the concrete walls that I had erected to define myself: Walls of a "can do" attitude built with bricks of impatience, pressure, force of will, self-sufficiency, and an identity based upon the walls I was able to maintain. Only the fullness of the Spirit of God was sufficient to refill my empty state, overcome my walls, and transform the dry vessel of my soul into streams of living water.

"'Whoever believes in me, as the Scripture has said, 'streams of living water will flow from within him.' By this he meant the Spirit, whom those who believed in him were later to receive"

(John 7: 38–39a).

RELEASE

The water has broken over the dam.
The wall that has held back the flow has been breached.
And I have found that the wall of the damming is myself.
The waters of my filling are God.
Set free from the stagnant backwater self,
My cup overflows with joyful, leaping, splashing, living water,
Making reservoir boundaries invisible and irrelevant,
Flowing together to fill the thirsty earth,
With rivers of living water,
That are God.

"We are only clay, but we carry within us the breath of God." [25]

TREASURE IN CLAY POTS

How strange to angels we must be,
Part spirit, part biology,
Performing in discrepancy
A truly divine comedy.
Set not in heaven, nor in hell,
But found in scenes of both to dwell,
Our soul's desire for perfection
Cast in a carnal misdirection.
The inner, constant, confrontation,
Epic conflict of creation,
Fought ceaselessly toward confusion,
War with no logical conclusion.
Until in divine recognition,
Soul kneels, ascending his condition;
And undeserving earthly sod
Turns temple for most Holy God.

CHAPTER 3

RESURRECTION

Passing through death brings us to the next important landmark on our journey, resurrection. After entering into the death of his false self, the wayfarer is raised to "live in spirit"[26] cleansed and free, with his "soul naked before God,"[27] much as St. Francis was described as emerging from his literal dark cave of prayer, wherein "prayer had eaten away his flesh again but what remained shone like pure soul."[28] This resurrection is the rebirth of the Spirit, which Jesus explained to Nicodemus (John 3:3). It is the initial reunion of the inner self with the Spirit of God accompanied by the continual call to deeper union as one moves along the Way. For the new Christian convert, this passage of new birth is usually symbolized by baptism, which "begins the climb…liberated from…slavery to death."[29] Here is now one who has become reborn into the open, innocent, unself-conscious, expectant nature of a child, who is able "to be touched—who can always learn and turn and begin again."[30] Here is the newborn ready for life.

"The last breath of Jesus breathed the Spirit into a new humanity. When we receive the Spirit, we receive the first glance of Jesus' new life."[31]

BORN AGAIN

I breathe in Your Spirit
And breathe out your life.
In the womb, I have lived
Without breath.
Let me be born,
Into the breath of life.
Call me forth,
And I will come through the water,
Lift my head
And gasp for Breath.
Release me from the cord of flesh
And fill me with your Breath of Life.
Breathing in, I am at peace.
Breathing out, I smile.

Jesus read the Holy words that described him, saying,

> The Spirit of the Lord is upon me,
> Because he has anointed me
> To preach good news to the poor.
> He has sent me to proclaim freedom for the prisoners And recovery of sight for the blind,
> To release the oppressed.

Luke 4:18

The one who is willing to step boldly into the light that reveals and transforms is confronted with death to the false self: a scary proposition! But with that death comes blessed annihilation of the fear and dread that has held the true self captive for so long. And then, resurrection to new life!

THE LIBERATION OF HANNAH

I participated in a controversially exhausting and spiritually uplifting experience for about five hours today. Hannah is a beautiful African American woman with an equally beautiful nine-year-old daughter. Hannah's daughter is quite brilliant. Hannah has a learning disability and is painfully shy. She has a heart of gold though she has undergone much abuse in her life. Recently her daughter has become terribly infested with head lice. And recently our school system has come under strict regulations that anyone found with lice must have a medical note from a nurse certifying that they are clean before they can return to class. Hannah has tried valiantly to get the nits out of her child's thick hair only to be turned back to work on it some more. Her child has thus been missing school and Hannah has not able to return to our classes either, (where an outbreak of lice has also begun.) She has had to stay home with her daughter. Since the rules require that all heads must be checked whenever there is an outbreak, we now have to certify that Hannah, as well as her daughter, is free from infestation in order for each of them to return to their respective classes: Hannah to Adult Literacy and her daughter to elementary school. Hannah has no transportation so I drove her and her daughter to the nurse to be checked. The daughter was checked and found to be still officially infested. But Hannah was too shy to submit to the nurse's inspection of her head. However, she did suggest that she would like to treat her own hair as well as her daughter's to ensure that they could both get a clean note and return to classes as soon as possible. It is nearly impossible to treat one's own hair. So I got a new kind of gentle treatment kit, bought lunch for the three of us, and we went to our center (there was no class going on at the time) to treat their hair myself. (That's the controversial part. "You did that at our center?!")

Over a period of talking with Hannah about this problem and these policies, Hannah confided in me that she was ashamed to have her head checked because she had large bald spots. Her hair was not real. (Recall that Hannah was abused as a child.) She asked that no one but me be present at the center for treatment of her hair. I reassured her and empathized with the anguish she must have been feeling from all of this. Her removal of her kerchief to reveal her head may be the bravest thing I've seen anyone do. She had to come to a point of total trust and submission. When I washed and carefully combed and treated her hair, she saw that I was in no way repulsed by the bald spots she so feared to reveal. We talked and actually had a nice time visiting. I then worked on her daughter's hair for several hours. When we were done, I asked Hannah if she would be able to let the nurse look at her hair, as well as her daughter's, to make the required checks. She smiled and said, "Yes, now I can."

She had been hiding this secret for the three years she had been in our program. It wouldn't have mattered to any of us anyway though it surely mattered to her. But when she revealed what she once had perceived to be shameful, her fear was conquered and she became free. She began to participate in social outings with her friend (a beautiful woman of color who was from Holland, full of confidence, who came to our program to work on her English skills). And she has been excited about starting our church's Saturday Bible study classes. The day-long event caused several "important" administrative reports to be turned in late. But I will never regret, nor forget, that liberating day spent with Hannah.

"There is no way one can tell people that they are walking around shining like the sun."[32]

Thomas Merton

In the *Wizard of Oz,* Dorothy believes she could find her heart's desire if only she could go "over the rainbow." But through her adventures in that faraway land she learns that her real heart's desire is to be surrounded by those who know and love her most of all. That place of reality and belonging is her true home. Likewise, when we have traveled through the valley of the shadow of death and come finally into the light of new life, we realize that the love, acceptance, and joy that we long have sought have been there for us all along. There in the light, love, and joy of God, we know that finally we *are* home. And as Dorothy has so famously said, "There's no place like home!"

REFLECTIONS OF LOVE

She grew up with little, and learned to survive.

Not with dolls or birthday parties, but with cunning, effective deceit and suspicion.

She learned to stay alive, as she was she was supposed to be.

Then she went out to learn and learned she was bad.

Not with joy and friends, but with hatred and judgment, She ran from the pain, fled disappointment, and became the failure she was never meant to be.

She found it painful to cope with her situation,

Not with acceptance and appreciation, but with punishment and isolation,

She took acceptance in any form to substitute for being loved, as she was supposed to be.

She became a mate and then a mother,

Not with showers of joy and acceptance, but with domination and ridicule,

As she became, she believed what everyone always said she would only be.

She came in chains and mistrust,

Not with anticipation and excitement, but with dread and desperation

To try to salvage a young life, determined to be more than she was culturally relegated to be.

She met loving ones, who reflected an unearthly light
Not with judgment and criticism, but with unconditional love,

That illuminated for her a glimpse of the beloved child she was created to be.

She worked tentatively, and met with some success
Not with furious competitiveness and quick achievement, but with slow and tiny upward steps.

And she almost believed she could be the success she always wanted to be.

She made mistakes and fell backwards in her progress
Not with "bounce-back" confidence, but with sad acceptance of her expected failure,

And she looked to the reflectors to see if they now saw what she was really only meant to be.

She saw in their unearthly light, a still more unearthly reflection
Not of failure or even grand ideals of achievement, but of steadfast, unconditional love.

And she saw an even more brightly illuminated image of the beloved child she hoped to be.

She ventured out a little farther, willing to risk a little more,

Not with dread and isolation, but with trust and anticipation (and the even the hint of joy).

And she began to glimpse her own image as that of the beloved child she sought to be.

She began to reflect some light herself, of an unearthly form

Not of glitter or of a false shine, but of love,

As she saw herself becoming the loving mother and beloved child she was always meant to be.

She then met the One who was the source of the light, and her reflection became bright,

Not of love she craved or sought or earned, but of love that had always been, just for her.

And she saw, in that light from above, below, and within, the beloved child she had always been.

"Someone touched me; I know that power has gone out from me" (Luke 8: 46).

We take our first steps of resurrected life with our Lord not in halls of perfect glory, but in dusty streets of clamoring humanity. But even in the midst of the needs and stresses that crowd and press against us, we have only to reach out in faith toward the Giver of Life and know that we can receive power and healing even through the merest touch of His garment.

TOUCH THE EDGE OF HIS CLOAK

Approach the towering, outspread branches of the tree of Life.

Breathe the soft, damp air of My Spirit.

Listen to the insistent rhythms of my evening song.

Feel the wet, cool grass that clothes my sleeping earth.

Gaze upon the incandescent moon and the million diamond stars.

Observe the limitless expanse of blue black velvet sky.

Touch the edge of My cloak

And be healed.

Once, having been asked by the Pharisees when the kingdom of God would come, Jesus replied, "The kingdom of God does not come with your careful observation, [21] nor will people say, `Here it is,' or `There it is,' because the kingdom of God is within you."

Luke 17:20–21 (NIV)

As the resurrection power of God brings light to the ends of the earth, the Kingdom of God is found breaking out in the most surprising places. The light has shone from the crude manger bed of an infant King to the morning light that illuminated an empty Easter tomb, from the Pentecostal fire that flamed in the hearts of the new church, to people of every nation, young, old, rich, poor, male, and female. And the light of resurrected life continues to shine in the most unlikely places carried by the most unlikely lanterns: even regular folk like you and me.

MARY'S SHOES

Mary began working with our company as a volunteer in our childcare area. She had such a magic touch with the children, that we hired her at the first opportunity. Despite her many gifts, Mary was very self-conscious. But she began to trust us as friends and took a leap of faith when she went to a resort town to participate with us in a statewide training conference. This sort of business travel was new for Mary, so she was very concerned about her apparel being appropriate. (It was.)

After walking in town one afternoon, her feet became sore due to her new shoes. Several of her coworkers offered her their loose sandals to help relieve her discomfort. But she wasn't able to wear them. Her friends suggested that she simply take off her shoes and walk barefoot. But she felt too embarrassed. She was going to leave the group and go back to her room. Her friends, seeing her distress, bent down and each of them took off their own shoes so that she could take hers off without feeling self-conscious or alone. She then joined the barefoot brigade and everyone had a wonderful afternoon together. No one who did this act thought it very significant. They simply loved her and wanted to help. Upon returning to the hotel, Mary came and told me the story of what her friends had done for her. She could not understand why anyone would treat her so well. But she did know that her friends were Christians. And so, right at that moment, Mary began to ask about what that meant. We read the Gideon's Bible and we talked, and prayed at her request. We continue to pray with and for her and her family as they learn to walk in freedom on the road to Life. But I don't think she will get a clearer lesson on Christ's own identification with our human state than she did when her friends stood and walked with her in willing, barefoot solidarity.

"'Greetings, you who are highly favored! The Lord is with you.'

Mary was greatly troubled at his words and wondered what kind of greeting this might be."

Luke 1:29

SEASON'S GREETINGS

What manner of greeting is this?
That the lowly of earth host the birth of our God?
What manner of greeting is this?
That earth, humble and empty with no seed yet planted,
Receives in its womb the earth Son of Creation
To be able to hold the One holding the earth?
What manner of greeting is this?
That earth, empty, barren, far past bearing fruit,
Paves the way of new life for all living oppressed,
To prepare blinded eyes for the dawn from on high?
What manner of greeting is this?
That all are invited to sit at the table,
Being filled with good things from the hands of a
Savior
To be able to live in the peace of His love?
What manner of greeting is this?
That the poor and the humble are freely exalted
Receiving full share from the bread that is broken
To be able to live in the light of God's favor?
What manner of greeting is this?
That the prisoners are called to abandon their prisons

Hearing truth that God's grace provides all that is
needed
To live trusting like children without worldly burden?
What manner of greeting is this?
That life offered to all passes through crucifixion
Losing life of the earth and bonds of human nature
To receive the new nature sprung from grace of God's
Spirit?
What manner of greeting is this?
That the lowly of earth host the birth of our God?
Receiving through death, the true nature of Life,
To live on the earth as the body of Christ
To be filled and to fill all those who are hungry
To receive and to share the bread that is broken
To live and proclaim that God's grace has provided
New life in God's Kingdom through the power of Love.

The life that God gives us through the death and resurrection of Jesus is life that is sure and eternal. Once that life is born anew in our spirit, we may contend with the forces of death. But the resurrected life and love of Jesus our Christ, our rock and our firm foundation, will have the last word.

I was walking stunned on the day of 9/ 11/ 01. I was in the halls of my seminary. And I didn't know what to feel. Hatred? Fear? Revenge? Anger? I found myself walking beside a friend, a brother in Christ who shared some classes with me. I said to him blankly, "I don't know how to feel." He answered with the most poignant and appropriate answer a Christian brother could have given, an answer that I must admit with some shame had not yet occurred to me. He said simply, "Feel love." Amen.

THE GREATEST OF THESE ...

The forces of death said,
"Come, let us overtake more territory.
For the time is right.
The access is ours.
Let us level their temples,
Crush their impotent gods,
And tear down the altars
Upon their high places.
Then they will be scattered,
Their faith proven vain.
Their hope will be lost.
Only death will remain."
So, they leveled the dwellings
Once thought to be temples,
Crushed the impotent powers,
Once followed as gods,
And tore down the altars,
Once upon the high places,
Leaving death in their wake ...
But death did *not* remain.
We, who once were scattered,
Realized our connection.

Faith, once buried, erupted,
Bearing fruit from the seed.
And hope that had smoldered,
Flamed forth from the ashes.
Indivisible Spirit,
Death merely revealed
For it could not destroy,
Past the former facade,
Faith's object,
Hope's source,
Living Love of our God.

"The thief comes only to steal and kill and destroy; I have come that they may have life, and have it to the full."

John 10:10

CHAPTER 4

LIFE

The final landmark on our metaphoric map of the Way is having "life to the full" (John 10:10). Having been reborn, or stripped down to "our true nature made in the likeness of God," we are compelled and enabled to live in the fullness of God's spirit of love. [33] We are called away from former self-centeredness into fulfillment of the shared life "on and on and on beyond all these practical things, to the goodness of the whole of life and (our) responsibility to it."[34] As we begin to live into our newly rediscovered sense of reality and purpose, we are astonished and humbled to realize that "We are only clay, but we carry within us the breath of God."[35] We have been filled to over-flowing so that the living abundance of the Spirit of God begins to flow out through us into all the earth to water a dry and thirsty land. In an extravagant and divine paradox, we are filled through the continual emptying spirit of self-surrender. Through the emergent reality of our inner strength that is the naked spark of God within us, we are able to "grasp life with both hands and then, with a leap of freedom, let go of it in order to be enveloped by its deeper mystery."[36]

"God is closer to us than we are to ourselves, and understanding this is to realize that God unifies everyone through the divine presence within us."[37]

Saint Augustine

I AM

God who sparkles quietly in the evening starlight,
Who smiles in the soft blush of morning,
Who walks and leaps in the grace of the deer,
Who fills the earth with flowers and trees and owls and ants,
God who is extravagant with thistles and ticks (why ticks, Lord?)
I long for deep union. I cry out to you and you answer,
"I am here."
I long to rest in your embrace and you answer,
"I embrace you; I am here."
I long to be filled with your Spirit and you answer,
"Breathe; I am here."
God, creator of extravagant life,
I need you to be
Loving me, holding me, filling me,
I cry out to you.
You answer eternally,
"I am."

"The idea is, not to take us out of the world, but to realize that God is in the world around us."[38]

Once I told my two-year-old that Jesus was living in his heart. His eyes grew large and he quickly responded, "Get Him out of there!" I wonder if we, too, don't sometimes tend to imagine the life that God gives as something we can put aside until church day, or until the next time we might need to call on God for a favor? But the good news is that the life of God is ever present, ready to fill us and draw us near to our Source and our Strength no matter where we are or what we are doing. Jesus brings us life that is real and eternal in the midst of all we do and of all we are. And that truth transforms even our most mundane of chores into genuine acts of highest holy worship.

DAILY COMMUNION

How Lord,
Amidst dirty dishes and unmade beds
Dare you come to me?
Why Lord,
Beyond doubt and death within my soul
Do you burn hot, and living?
What Lord,
Makes you sacrifice divinity,
Glory to my sin?
Where Lord,
Can I offer appropriate praise,
And love for You?
Who Lord,
Suffers Hell for me when I deserve
That killing flame?
Yes Lord,
I will make the bed and wash the dishes
And live and love and move and breathe,
In Love with you,
Alive in you,
Forever.

"A man who does not wonder is like a pair of spectacles behind which there are no eyes." [39]

Thomas Carlyle

A LOVE SONG

He fills me like a sparkling mountain stream.
A voice that stills me, I hear like echoes of a dream.
His presence thrills me. Although I hurt Him every day,
Yet still He wills me to walk beside Him on the Way.
Jesus, fill me up with your power.
You condescended to love me from heaven's holy tower;
Could have ascended above me, but you held out your hand,
And said, "Come with me, if you love me, to my Father's promised land."
Jesus, I'm unworthy in my sin.
But you can change me from my tortured heart within.
And you'll still love me, although I fail you once again.
I reach above me and grasp your waiting hand, my Friend.

"People only become fully human when they are received and accepted." [40]

Henri Nouwen

When we open our hearts, souls, eyes, and ears to the life of God, we get glimpses of his radiant glory and moments of heavenward transcendence even as we live and breathe day by day. As the dividing walls that had kept us from knowing God, ourselves, and one another begin to crumble, we are privileged to rare and beautiful glances of life in God's reality that goes beyond "a poor reflection as in a mirror," offering a brief and exciting preview of the truth we shall one day see, "face to face" (1 Corinthians 13: 12).

JAM SESSION

In a refurbished colonial tavern in a small West Virginia town, after the attached store has closed and the light of day has faded, folks begin to gather as they can, by ones, twos, and occasionally groups of three or more. Some have musical instruments, some do not. Chairs and benches of every sort are pulled into a large circle where the gathering persons sit. Musicians take out their instruments and begin to tune and adjust them. There are dulcimers, guitars, banjos, fiddles, flutes, and perhaps even more exotic fare, depending on who is in town on this night. There will be professionals, amateurs, singers, and listeners of every age and description. Those who are not working to prepare their instruments are, perhaps, talking quietly to their neighbors. But there is a reverent sense of quiet expectation. There is a peace and calm that pervades the gathering, which no one wants to disturb.

Then at some mutually agreed upon moment, when enough have gathered and are prepared, the music begins. It is a music of beautifully blended equality, empathetic unity, and unique individuality. Each musician has his own sound, his own gift, his own specialty that he brings to the whole. Together the music flows into melodies that none could make alone, but which highlights the particular sound of each musician. And the musicians listen to one another and join where the music invites them to join. It is communication and reciprocation and mutual affection and appreciation. And we who listen know that this is authentic and will never be exactly duplicated. That is part of the joy of the moment.

On the night I attended, an invitation spontaneously evolved for each of the musicians to not only play, but to sing a favorite song that all those gathered could join. Each musician offered a selection around the circle, which they taught or began, and we all were invited to sing together. I learned later that this was a rare occurrence, having all present be a part of actually making the music. But it fostered such a sense of unity and understanding that I felt I was coming to know every person there in a way that went beyond casual conversation of words and formalities. When folks had to begin leaving the session, it seemed like a sad farewell. When we left, I felt folks would miss us as well.

We returned to our place of residence with a feeling of satisfied peace and even joy.

We had recognized a connection between us.

And it was good.

We had felt a mutual affection.

And it was good.

We had glimpsed a force of love beyond us that flowed within and among us.

And it was God.

"If we build the Jesus-life in our own souls, we can see God where God is. Everywhere."[41]

Joan Chittiser

PEACE

His peace washes over me
With the gentle cleansing of a warm spring rain.
It seeps into my soul
As the present joy of bird song penetrates the conscious-
ness of the quiet mind.
It permeates my being
With the subtle sweetness of honeysuckle on the
breeze;
And satisfies my hunger
Like the warm tranquility of mother's milk nourishes her
baby.
It renews my heart
With the hope and joy of the wanderer who finally sees
his home.
His peace He gives.
Be still and know, in every sense, that He is God.

"But when they became fully awake, they saw his glory."

Luke 9:32

AWAKE AT MAMIE'S

I remember as a child the magical freedom that I felt as I awoke in my grandmother and grandfather's house, Mamie and Big Tam's. It was a peaceful awakening that came gently with the early morning breeze through the two, long, raised windows on the west side of the house. I slept there (on these very special holidays at Mamie's) in the nurturing comfort of a real feather bed covered with handmade cotton sheets and quilts. As I opened my eyes to the reliable call of the rooster, I listened dreamily to the soothing rhythm of the Mourning Dove. He seemed to call me gently to come and join in the completely safe and limitless joy that lay ahead on this magical day. My awakening mind and body began to hear other birds joining his minor key with faster, higher notes, and to breathe the softly intoxicating smell of summer honeysuckle. Then as I came to hear also, the practical and busy clucking and crooning of the hens in their nearby barnyard, I heard the altogether comforting sounds of Mamie, humming and padding around in her house shoes preparing for me breakfast.

Everything in that house was real. The coffee was

brewed with well water on the stove. The biscuits were baked by the fuel of wood in cast iron. The eggs were fresh from the nests of reluctant hens. The floors were smooth wood, covered with large, flat woolen rugs. Life moved with the rhythm of the earth, waking with the sun, and resting with its setting. Meals were for nourishment and were taken from the very earth that God had entrusted into their care. There was a pond for fishing, and time to fish. And the bigger fish were eaten. There was a creek for wading, and time to wade. There was a barn filled with dried corn that made a wonderful slide. (Though it itched afterward—but then there was *Calamine* lotion for that.) There were wooden smokehouses filled with hanging meats and gardens growing with every kind of vegetable. There were cows and goats and chickens, guineas, cats, and a little bouncy dog. There were bluffs and woods where one could find Indian arrowheads, rattlesnakes (so we always heard), and grapevines for swinging. I always told my friends that my grandparents were rich. As far as I could see, they had everything anyone could ever want. And once during my visit, I was allowed to go to McClellan's and choose any one toy from the long wooden toy counter.

Anything, my choice! Yes, they were definitely rich. (I chose the baby doll, though I've always kind of longed for the silver dress-up shoes that I left behind.)

Big Tam was, ironically, a very short little blue-eyed man of Irish descent. He was the embodiment of the peace and quiet joy that permeated his home. He did the shopping and brought the bounty home for Mamie. He drove an old, green, round-fendered Ford pick-up truck with bouncy, worn, brown leather seats. If there were seatbelts, I don't remember them. He was a man of regular and devout prayer. Every prayer that I ever heard him pray ended with "Lord, make us 'umble and lovable." I can attest (as can anyone who knew him) that the Lord answered his prayer. He called me "Joy" instead of Joyce. He was the only person to call me that, and I have always treasured his reference to me. For at his and Mamie's house, I *was* joy. Each morning brought with it the hope of adventure and opportunity to experience the joy that is the cadence of life lived in reality, without false fronts or imposed constraints.

Mamie was an amazing contrast to Big Tam. She was tall and brown and of Native American descent. She could be very strong willed and (so I've heard) even harsh at times. She had a no-nonsense outlook on life. She insisted that things be done right. But she also had a surprising, even mischievous sense of humor that was lovely to see. Mamie worked as hard as Big Tam and she pretty well felt that she "ruled the roost." She had a great love for nature, and she often took me on nature walks during which she would point out and identify wild flowers, birds, animals, insects, special rocks, and Indian arrowheads. Mamie could kill a rattlesnake with a rock and a hoe. And she very often did. She kept a loaded shotgun behind the door, and she knew how to use it. Mamie was fearless, except for the fear of losing of her independence. (Which she did, in the end, and then she even overcame that fear.)

This morning I took a moment to sit on my front porch swing. I heard the Mourning Dove, felt the gentle breeze, and breathed the sweetness of honeysuckle carried upon it, and I remembered life as Joy.

What if we awakened to receive life spread out before us like the bright gifts on McClellan's toy counter, ours for the choosing? What if we were to awake and see that our sleep is over, and breakfast has been lovingly prepared for us to receive? What if we opened our eyes to receive the reality of life as Joy?

What if we don't?

CHAPTER 5

THE CONTINUING CYCLE OF LIFE

There is an unfortunate assumption on the part of some who enter upon the path to life that the transformative steps on the way to life: *truth, death, resurrection, and life* are a one-time occurrence. But those who continue upon this journey toward life in the Spirit soon learn that Christianity is "not *merely* life after death, but *death and resurrection present in every moment of human experience.*" Death and resurrection are immediate experiences, not just ultimate events.[42] It is through the continuing cycle of truth leading to conviction and death leading to resurrected unity and recommitment that we "transform daily dying with freely chosen love."[43] The apostle Paul said, "I die every day" (1 Corinthians 15:31). Our deepening union with God leads to an increasing hunger for such union and an increasing realization of our need for God's transforming holiness. And thus we are pulled upward toward a spiral of transforming love. This upward progression begins with our first communion with God and continues until we are fully transformed into the glory and likeness of the One we seek, and who seeks us. St. Augustine describes this upward spiral beautifully:

> You have blazed forth with light and have shone upon me, and you have put my blindness to flight! You have sent forth fragrance and I have drawn in my breath and I pant after you. I have tasted you and I hunger and thirst after you. You have touched me, and I have burned for your peace.[44]

By the end of my final full year at seminary, I was exhausted. I had tried valiantly to pretend that I could do everything, parent four children (the fifth one had not yet arrived), run a family literacy program, keep up a household, hold an active role in my church, and get a full seminary degree. I didn't want to burden anyone with what I perceived to clearly be *my* work. Though I couldn't have survived without the ongoing help that so many had given, I *had* managed my *pretense* of invincibility so well that when I wrote this poem my husband looked at me in astonishment and said, "You're tired?" Lord, help me to admit my own weakness so I can be strengthened fully by the life that You give.

"Take it; this is my body." Matthew 14:22

RESURRECTED

The Cry

Father, I'm tired.

I'm worn out and tired.

I'm searching for how to be able to rest.

I've done very many things, but none too well, I fear.

And I wonder, are my deeds worth their inherent sacrifice?

Am I working to please others, to satisfy ego, to prove my own worth?

Where do I stop? And where do I start? And whom do I ask? And when do I rest?

When do I walk forward? Where do I stand firm? How do I retreat and where do I advance?

The Body Given

I asked for your heart,
And I fear You have answered with love so enormous, so
strongly compelling
That my weak human nature cannot bear the strain.
So I ask You to crucify my selfish nature,
Birth fully in all parts, even parts darkly hidden,
Your own super nature, your own perfect peace.
I asked for your eyes
And I fear You have answered with light so revealing I'm
cut to the core,
And I can't close my eyes to your truth anymore.
So I ask for your wisdom
Born of humble acceptance
With love that sees all with right judgment and mercy.
I asked for your hands
And I fear You have answered with a task far too great
For my own failing strength.
So I ask for your faith
That will through You move mountains,
Heal that which is broken, make impossible, real.
I asked for your feet

And I fear You have answered with a journey too won-
derful, high in your glory,
A journey too terrible, dark in death's valley,
That I faint to move through it, and fear the next step.
So I ask for true ears
To discern your quiet call,
To hear as You guide me in ways not my own.
Lord, I asked for your body,
And I fear You have answered with so great a love that I
can't bear the strain,
With such high sacrifice, that I can't look away:
Your own body to break
To nourish my weakness
And restore to full life on the path You have trod,
All who would follow the way You provide
That leads us to life through the love of our God.
The Body Resurrected
I will sleep in your peace, and rise in the morning,
To life that is new in your glory and grace,
Receiving your life blood,
Poured out for my strength,
Receiving your body,
Broken for my bread,
I will listen to follow

In your perfect way,
I will rest
In the peace, of your faithful assurance,
I will look with your eyes,
Seeing truth through your mercy,
I will live
In and through and filled up with your love,
Reborn of your spirit,
Nourished with your body,
Refilled with your love,
I will walk in your Way.
Amen

"But when you give a banquet, invite the poor, the crippled, the lame, the blind, [14] and you will be blessed. Although they cannot repay you, you will be repaid at the resurrection of the righteous."

Luke 14:13

NEW TABLE ETIQUETTE

What would happen if we who have been blessed with the full life of Jesus our Lord were to begin to really live out His teaching? What if we invited folks to the table who had great need? It sounds lovely—even holy. So I thought, Let's do it!

I worked in a government grant program that attempted to illuminate the way toward full life for victims of poverty, under-education, and disability by bringing them the light of learning. It seemed very natural to seek to locate this program within a church. And the doors appeared to swing wide open. The church certainly wanted to help the poor, who they knew must exist, in theory, out there, some-where. Theories are nice to talk about and even plan for. ... but it is hard to actually hear or love (or despise) a theory. A theory also does not smell bad, sport chains and tattoos, and does not ask for money, diapers, formula or a place to hide from a dangerous spouse. Theories are not too dangerous. And they are not too real or hungry. The program was invited into the walls—in theory. And then theory became real. This is what happened.

Church: Look at our beautiful temple—I mean church. You can't keep those baby beds and toddler toys out where people can see them. You can't move that furniture. It messes up the symmetry of the room! Why is our Sunday school classroom holding books in messy bookcases? They're taking up our fellowship space. Why have you taken up some of our closet space? That's where the games and supplies for the church folk go. This looks tacky. This is God's house, not a gathering place for poor people and children! (Then it was the government's turn from whence we had received the grant to operate.)

Government: Yes, we did award you a new grant. It is a wonderful program. But, we've changed our minds. Money is short. And we can't be making improvements to church property anyway. So we're taking our money back. Unless you can change your class set-up to suit our new rules you will lose the money we promised.

Church: No. We will not bend. We will structure the classes as we have them, and we will not be told how to run our long-established child care program that serves the very best families in this community. We hate to see these poor kids suffer because of

governmental stupidity, but if they have to suffer because of our principles, then so be it.

Government: The program must go.

Program: Can we ask the congregation for help? Is this an outreach of the church?

Church: Yes. But we refuse to give any money to it—on principle, (the principle being that the government should pay for this and not the church).

Program: Can we have a minute to speak to the congregation about this mission?

Church: Well.....this is an outreach of the church—but ... then silence.

People of Church: What program? Why is this furniture moved? We have some kind of poor people program?

Postscript: There were no free infant care facilities in our community, which was what most of our families needed in order to secure their basic education. So the staff tried to continue the program without government funding. The church willingly sponsored three children part time in their existing nursery school. (But no money was offered for other salaries or supplies.) The rest of the program stayed on for a year by cutting services and collaborating with other programs for some salaries. Some staff simply volunteered to work for no pay at all. But eventually the program could not continue without monetary support, and it closed. Few people in the church had even known that the program had existed there. Many of those who did were not sad to see it go.

Now, when you open the door, and make a place at the table, who is the object of this mission? Is it the hungry one being welcomed to the table, or is it the one who has to move down out of the place of honor, swallow his pride, and welcome the possibly pungent newcomer to sit with him in equality and full communion? What about the one who has to share his hard-earned daily bread with this empty-handed, unemployed person, coming hungry to the table? And who would we find serving at such a table? Perhaps in such a communion our eyes would be opened, and we would see the presence of the One who has invited all to come and be nourished by the very bread and life blood of His body, which we are to become. Through communion and community, the Body of Christ lives out the Kingdom come. Lord, help us. This can't be done.

"With man, it is impossible. But with God, all things are possible" (Matthew 19:26). Messy business, this new table etiquette.

Through faith we are empowered to "Grasp life with both hands and then, with a leap of freedom, let go of it in order to be enveloped by its deeper mystery." [45]

Once while working in a chaplaincy program that I needed to complete my seminary training, I complained about the constant state of transition in which my life seemed to move. There was a retired gentleman in our training group who was an experienced psychologist. I valued his wisdom and his life experience. So I asked him, "When does this life transition stuff stop?" He responded honestly and wisely with copious peals of hearty laughter! I got the point.

UNFINISHED POEM

I was tired and hungry
And trying to follow the way that led
Into the dark uneasy night.
I was feeling confused,
As much as convicted about the unsure way
That led over dark waters.
Small, weak, hungry,
And confused I stood before the precipice
Of your insistent, unsettling, frightening will.
How could I walk forward?
Straight into nothing,
Stepping on nothing?

Now a man came up to Jesus and asked, "Teacher, what good thing must I do to get eternal life?"

Matthew 19:16

THE RICH MAN'S SECOND CHANCE

Here's the story.

On Sunday I preached a sermon about the rich man and the eye of the needle. It was a convincing sermon. Well done, thought I. Funny though, my own pastor seemed to present me to my home congregation (to whom I delivered the message) as someone who was about to go off to some new adventure just because I'm about to finish seminary? He seemed to treat this as my swan song. *What's he think he's doing?* I don't have time to think about that now. I barely have time to think. I have very many commitments that keep me hopping every second. And I can't possibly let them go. We need money. I need *some* sort of stability.

On Monday I wandered and moped through my commitments. I didn't want to admit the stress I'd been feeling lately. Nothing seemed to fit just right anymore. I love being a teacher. I *am* a teacher. And that is a ministry. And that is certainly enough. It helps others. It helps pay the bills. It's what I do. And yet, something was not right. Sure, God called me into ministry. But I could not possibly even think of doing another thing! I said, "I need guidance, God. I don't know where I'm going or where you want me to go. I need to pray." So between commitments, I went to a park and sat on a rock in a mountain stream.

And I saw that the stream was a living thing, a creative thing. And I saw that the life was in the movement. The creativity was in the process. What was the water producing? Could I see a product? Not immediately. The beauty of the stream was in the movement of all the water. I couldn't see any one drop of water. I couldn't say, stand still and let me examine you. Stand here or there and be water. The nature of the water in this stream was to move with the contours of the land. The contours of the land imposed some limits on the stream. But the stream also imposed subtle and lasting changes on the contours of the land. The water and the land were part of each other.

I realized the creativity here is the process. And the process is ongoing. I thought about how the water moving in a stream has an attraction for us, offering a serene and living peace that flows with its movement. And this attraction is, strangely, much the same as the attraction we have to fire. We watch and are attracted by the process of fire. Can we stop a single flame? Can we examine and know a tongue of fire? No, the beauty of fire is in its process. It burns and steadily changes its fuel. In the process we feel the effects, warmth and light. There is a product, ash. But most of us don't burn a fire to get the ash. We burn a fire to receive the warmth and light that emanate from the burning, the process of fire. And it is the same with wind. Wind is even defined by its movement. If the air did not move, there would be no wind. We enjoy the soft kiss of a gentle breeze due to the process of movement. Entire landscapes are changed by the movement of wind, water, and fire. The water and fire of the atmosphere cycle in tandem with the movement of wind.

"The wind blows wherever it pleases. You hear its sound, but you cannot tell where it comes from or where it is going. So it is with everyone born of the Spirit" (John 3: 8).

Then I asked, "What does this mean?" And it seemed to me that life is process, not product. Life is in the living. We wouldn't stop a child from growing in order to keep him still at some point in childhood, to stop the growth and the change. To stop the building up and the breaking down—the very process of life—would mean death. Life is process. Creation is process, not product. Love is the same. Love is given, received, active. Can we stop love and look at the product? Is love the lover's diamond ring, the child's dandelion, or is it the living, growing process that prompts the giving of these symbols? What if we confuse the product with the process?

But aren't there legitimate products? Doesn't love, life, fire, wind, and water, in the process of its being, have the effect of creating new things—products? Perhaps we should say byproducts. The process is where the life exists, and the byproducts are fringe benefits, icing on the cake if you will.

I have lived a little while, and I have talked to folks who have lived quite a while. When was the process of life most exciting, most alive? So often I have found that the memories that bring joy to the heart are those that recall times when life was almost pure process, when everything persons had was put into the process of living, and there was little left over in the way of "byproducts."

My family recalls with great fondness the year we moved to a new place with no money, no connections, and no "safety net" for my husband's new job. We lived week to week. By the end of the month we literally ate pancakes. Our kids thought those were the most wonderful meals of all. We were pleased with our creativity and ability to make it together, through the process of living. For a time, we had few worldly attachments. It took all our resources to live. And so, we *lived!* We took the opportunity to go to the park, the beach, to watch the kids play outside, to go exploring around the town together. We were neither blessed nor burdened with many possessions. We were fully involved in the process of life, not the product. We were living creatively, fully, and enjoying the movement within the limits of our stream banks. Perhaps we even altered the places we moved over. But that was simply the outcome of the process, and not the object. We were living for the sake of life together.

Wind has a product. It breaks down rocks and moves earth. The effect is seen in piles and contours of soil. Moving water has a product. Look at the bars of sand and soil at the tail waters of streams. The movement produces mounds of soil. Fire has a product. The fuel is burned and changed and eventually disintegrates into ash—essentially a component of soil. Earthly life has a product. An eventual pile of bones that will break down and by wind, water, and fire become soil. "Ashes to ashes, dust to dust." The product is soil. So is that why we live? Is that why wind blows and fire burns and water flows? Is the object of it all the product? Are we destined only to accumulate and disintegrate into dirt?

The rich man had many products. He had lived life, a process. But he was distracted by the products and, perhaps, was a slave to their care. Jesus said, "Come join in the process of life. Come live in the life that is eternal within and yet beyond the making of more piles of earth. Come *now* into eternal *life*. Leave your burden of dead attachments. Come and follow me."

And the rich man "went away grieving for he had many possessions" (Matthew 19:22, NRSV).

I am the rich man. Okay, so I'm not a man and I'm not rich—so to speak. But I am a human and I do have many attachments. And the byproducts of the process of my life and the lives of those I love could become the object of my life. That's not going to happen though. Is it?

I sat on a rock and said, "God, what do you want me to do? What do I need to do to inherit eternal life?"

On Tuesday I went to class where I am learning about how to love others unconditionally and how to live into the process of being the hands and feet of Christ for others. The class is wonderful. I am growing. We are all growing together. The process is active and creative. There is building up, breaking down, and real movement. It is very good. And my teacher said, "Will you be able to enter fully into this process? Will you go toward the place this process will take you?"

And I said, "I have very many commitments. I have very many attachments. I must attend to them. This process is taking me away from them. So, no. I cannot continue." And I went away sorrowful.

On Wednesday, I attended to very many commitments. And I was not even able to attend well. My commitments were too many. I even left my child stranded at school. I was attending to one of my many commitments. I became frantic and lost and I said, "I can't do this!" Thank God for the final utterance of truth.

On Thursday I went to practice the process of loving others, of being the hands and feet of Christ. And it was good. But I told my mentor that I couldn't continue this process. I had very many commitments.

I had to be concerned about the products that my attachments would produce. I needed money. And I was out of energy too. I was becoming worn down. I had to stop this process. And my mentor said, "I invite you to release your heavy attachments in order to receive the new process of life to which God seems to be calling you." I said, "No, I'm not sure. I'm not ready. I don't know. I'm worn out I have to stop something."

On Friday I walked through God's creation. I thought about my dilemma. I knew I had to release something. I had initially chosen to leave the process that would cause more change, more growth, and the breaking down of what must be broken. It's a scary thing to be involved in such a process. And where will it lead? Who can stop a drop of water and say, "Where are you going? Stop and give me your plan!" If the drop pulled itself away behind a quiet rock it could be still. But it would become stagnant and old if it stayed there. I have been looking for a rock to hide behind, holding on to my former accomplishments, my former identity. *Haven't I been changed enough already? When does this end!* Can't I stay in this quiet pool and continue in my former lifestyle to the glory of God?

Must I let go of my recent re-attachment to this bit of lovely, comfortable earth here in this little eddy?"

On Saturday I received a call from a church to come and preach a trial sermon. If it goes well they could call me to be their pastor. It scared the hell out of me. I stammered and stumbled. I didn't say it. But I thought, *Wait! I'm not ready. How can I possibly hear this call? How can I possibly heed it? How can I possibly let go of the attachments that have protected me so well these many years?*

I said, "God, what do you want me to do? What do I need to do to inherit eternal life?"

But there is nothing more given than, "Come. Follow me."

I said, "There must be a more controlled and secure route to eternal life."

My answer is only, "Come. Follow me."

I said, "I don't know where you are going. How can I know the way?"

My answer was only, "I am the way. Come."

It is hard. But despite my hesitation, I sure am glad I got a second chance to take up the offer.

When I was in college and entering the joy of my increasingly adult life, I floated about on a cloud of confidence, sure that I had gained much important knowledge and a depth of wisdom that would propel me easily through life. But then I graduated and had to go to work. The more I learned and the more I lived, the more I realized how much I didn't know. When I prepared to have my first child I had all the best books and the expert advice memorized. My husband and I were certain that we had the fool-proof plan for perfect child rearing. That all-knowing euphoria lasted until the first night we were home from the hospital. It is much the same with our progression into genuine life of the Spirit. Our first step out of the darkness into the liberating joy of light begins the exciting journey where we are compelled to go "further up and further in,"[46] moving nearer to God's revealing and transforming light wherein we see all the more clearly our besetting sins and our need for further transformation. It is an ongoing process. A beautiful and terrible journey into light and life wherein "we, who with unveiled faces all reflect the Lord's glory, are being transformed into His likeness with ever-increasing glory, which comes from the Lord, who is the Spirit" (2 Corinthians 3:18).   Amen.

HERE I PRAY AGAIN

God, I need your help.

I find I'm not as loving as I thought I was.

And my pride—my self-righteousness—well it's still there.

God, I need your help.

I find I'm not as trusting as I thought I was.

And my false notion of self-sufficiency instead of God sufficiency. ... well it's still there.

God, I need your help.

I find I'm not as Spirit filled as I thought I was.

And my physical appetite with the will to satisfy it. ... well it's still there.

God, I need your help.

I find I'm not as faithful as I thought I was.

And my forgetfulness of your promises, your grace, and your word. ... well it's still there.

God, I need your help.

I find I'm not as longsuffering as I thought I was.

And my impatient shortsightedness born of self-centeredness ... well it's still there.

Oh God, how I need your help.

I find I'm not nearly as Christ like as I thought I was.

And my besetting sins … … Lord help me they're still there.

"What a wretched one I am! Who will rescue me from this body of death? Thanks be to God—through Jesus Christ our Lord!" (Romans 7:24–25).

God have mercy.

Christ have mercy.

Lord have mercy.

Thank you for forgiving me, 70 times 7 (and then some).

Thank you for transforming me.

Thank you for loving me and drawing me near.

But oh, Lord, the nearer I get to you, the brighter the light shines,

And the more clearly I see that

Oh God, I need your help.

ENDNOTES

1   By these words, Spanish poet Antonio Machado y Ruiz emphasizes the image of a journey.

2

3   Cunningham, Lawrence S. ed. *Thomas Merton and the Monastic Vision*, Grand Rapids: Eerdmans, 1999. p 182

4   Merton, Thomas. *Zen and the Birds of Appetite*, Abbey of Gethsamani, 1968. p 26

5   Merton, Thomas. *Spiritual Direction and Meditation*, Collegeville: The Liturgical Press, 1960. p 97

6   Merton, *Meditation* 72

7   Rice, Edward. *Man in the Sycamore Tree*, New York: Harcourt Brace, 1985. p 135

8   Merton, *Meditation* 99

9   Ryan, John K. *The Confessions of St Augustine*, New York: Doubleday, 1960. p 252

10   Larranga, Ignacio, 25.

11   Cunningham, *Monastic* 80

12   Nouwen, Henri. *Pray To Live: Thomas Merton: A Contemplative Critic.* Notre Dame, IN: Fides, 1972. p 70

13   Merton Zen 26

14   Merton, Meditation 90.

15   McDonnel, Thomas. "Interview With Thomas Merton." October, 1967. p 41

16   Chittister 205

17   Chittister 70

18   Merton, *Zen* 86

19   Chittister 204

20   Larranaga,. p 66

21   Cunningham, Lawrence S. ed. *Thomas Merton, Spiritual Master: The Essential Writings.* Mahwah, NJ: Paulist, 1992. p 296

22   Chittister 205

23   Chittister 195

24   Merton, *Seven* 325

25   Heagle 124

26   Merton, *Seven* 230

27   Cunningham, *Monastic* 182

28   Larranga Ignacio, O.F.M. CAP. *Sensing Your Hidden Presence*, Garden City, NY: Doubleday, 1987. p 19

29   Merton, Merton, Thomas. *The Seven Story Mountain*, New York: Harcourt Brace, 1948. p 221

30   Chittister, Joan. Wisdom Distilled from the Daily: Living the Rule of St. Benedict Today. Harper Collins, San

Francisco 1991. p 24

31   Heagle 128.

32   Merton, Monastic Vision, 69

33   Merton, *Seven* 372

34   Chittister, Joan, p 20

35   Heagle, John. *Life to the Full*, Chicago: Thomas More Press, 1976. p 124

36   Heagle 43

37   Cunningham, *Spiritual*. p. 169

38   Chittister 31

39   Heagle, 71

40   Nouwen, Henri. *Creative Ministry*, Redmond Washington: Paradoxal Press, 1991. p 33

41   Chittister 201

42   Heagle 118

43   Heagle 120

44   Ryan 254

45   Heagle 43

46   Lewis, C.S. *The Chronicles of Narnia: The Last Battle:* C.S. Lewis (PTC), 1956. p 198

INDEX OF POEMS AND NARRATIVES BY TITLE